Moments:

This to the Next

Poetry - Now and Eternity

Gary W. Burns

Turning Corner Books ™

WWW.TURNING CORNER BOOKS.COM

Other Books of Poetry
by Gary W. Burns

Bridges: To There
  (Poems for the Mind, Body & Spirit)

Clouds: On the Wind
  (Poems for the Soul – A Meditation)

Earth Tones: A Journey
  (Poetry for the Journey)

Garden Walks: Hand In Hand
  (Poems To Relax By)

Poems of Love: A Selection

Rainy Day: Wondering
  (Poems for a Rainy Day)

To You With Love: Selected Poems

Twilight: Awaking the Stars
  (Poems To the Night's Light)

To Jonathan

So many
Thanks

CONTENTS

⌘ ──────────────────────────────

A Point Called Time

Moments To Hours

⌘

Clocks and Faces

iii

Time – And You and Me

A Point Called Time

Today

Living
In darkened rooms

Webbed
By history

There's
Too little light
To see.

Come out,
And be
With me.

Truly,
Today

In Moments: This To the Next

Landscapes

At times,
Across the landscapes
Of our lives

There's sunny-yellow,
Lively-tangerine,
And fields-of-green.

Then,
Now and again,
There are moments-blue
And moments-gray.

And somehow,
Through it all,
There's dreamy-ebony
And lighthouse-white
Guiding our way.

The Hard Rains

While going through the park today
I took the time to notice the trees:

Intermittently, the rain came down
And at times
The green, the brown,
And the blue-gray of day
Blurred
And distinction went away.

At times
It rained so very hard.

But, as I
Moved along
Time went by

And slowly
The sun came out
Brightening the day,
And lighting the
                    Way.

In Your Solitude

In
The solitude
Of you
There's a soul
Moving slow
And ever easy.

A soul
Filled with beauty,
Warmth,
And kindness.

Ready
For the living
Desiring
The giving.

Come
From there
In your solitude.

A Calling

Love
Called my name;

I answered.

And
Here we are,

Love
And me

Calling.

Over the River Time

The lifetime's placed
The bridge is held

Spanning,
You to me
Me to you

Extending,
Then till now
Now till then

Spanning,
Always spanning

Over the river time

Fall
Clockworks

In the gust,

The old oak
Let go
A flock of leaves
And other flocks
Winged
From other trees.

In Our Going

I sit with you
By the edge of the sea

And waves of time
Keep coming,

And coming,
And coming:

In our going.

Looking Through

The window
To wonder,

Love.

Dearest
Song Bird

1
By late morning
The many birds
That sang at dawn
Are near on
Quiet.

Day,
By and by,
Brings noon
To loaf awhile.
And the birds
And their songs
Become quieter
Still.

2

In the heat
Of the hours
Close after noon
The woods are filled
With near silence.

3

Evening
Stills.

4

O Dear Song Bird,
Fill your morning
With song
For
In not too long
Morning's song
Is gone.

The Pair

The cardinals:

He,
Red
Against
Leaf green;

She,
Brown-gray
Amongst
Shade and limb.

Him
   forever
   bringing:
Her
   forever
   bearing.

The pair. . .

At Present

Off in the distance
There is
Something . . .

Distance future . . .
Distance past . . .

But at last,
Distance
Never comes.

Consequently,
Two are one,

At present.

As Eternity

As eternity
Is about
You and me;

No one
Is an island

That they
Are not the sea.

Starry Night

Gazing upon
The multitude of stars
I came to know

The universe
Is ours.

Deep,
Close,
The stars
And the host.

The sight;
Immortal dark
Clothed
In eternal light.

O starry night.

Moments to Hours

One Love

Morning was asked,
"Morning
Do you miss
     the night?"

Morning's light
Replied,
"I'm holding
   her hand;
      Love's
        grand."

Common Ground

All sought
Common ground,
In silence
It was found.

Strolling
With You

Strolling the boardwalk
At the edge
Of life,

Together,
We make our way
Along the afternoon.

Aria

1

Gallantly
The gray fog moves
In soft silent swirls
While drifting
Its wayward way through
The old narrow streets
Of Padua.

2

With the open air market
Gone for the day
And darkness near on
A man gray – with age
Sweeps with a fagot broom
Old worn cobbles
Which have escaped ruin.

3

Some-where-out-there
In night's omni-darkness
The wander gray soul
And the secular gray mist
Will come to rest
To await
The warmth of a new day
To ease them away.

Built

Built,
The bridge
    is crossed.

Somewhere

Somewhere
In the wind
Your name begins . . .

The Old Farm Pond

1

Across the old farm pond
Some geese
     walk guardedly
On today's,
      last night made,
         thin ice.

2

Others,
   like ice-breakers,
   lunge forth
       pushing
      breast-forward
Making watery ways
   for others
     to follow.

3

But none,
        no matter what,
                    get stuck.

They simply
            fly away.

4

Keep flying.

Be Still

1

If only
For
A little while
Now and then,
Be still.

2

Wait,
Be patient.

3

The bird
Is just a branch
Away.

Listen,
The singing is near.

Hear,
The song
Of peace ere long.

4

Be still,
If only

For
A little while

Now and then.

The Bridge
Called Journey

1

While
Crossing
The bridge
Journey -

2

Traveling
The road
Life

3

Walking
The sidewalk
Hope

4

Searching
Through the rain
Time

5

I find
My-
Self

In the arms
Of Love

6

Please
Join me

Across the Threshold

Both day and night,
Amongst a host
Of starry light,

Across the threshold
Time and space
The constellation
Self
Transfigures
You and me
Eternally.

This Moment Completely

The only place
You can't be lost;

This moment.

Be here
With me

Lovingly

In this moment
Completely.

Midnight Bright

Shhhh

Lay by me
Quietly

Our touch
Our knowing

Our warmth

Showing

The light that shines
Midnight bright

Love

In Love

While holding
Your kind hands
And softly kissing
Your tender lips
In bliss
We gently fell:
In love.

In Moments: This To the Next

Symmetry

Looking through
The minds eye
There's always
A window
To look out of
Or into.

The window
To the soul,
Perhaps.

A window
To the world,
Maybe.

Then again,
Truth may have it
That window

Be

You and me
Essentially.

Peace & Me

We met on a walk
Along the shore

Greeted one another
With a simple hello

Talked awhile, laughed,
And by way of love
Came to know
One another

And
In the grace of now
Are one
And the same:

Peace & me

Come along with us
Let's walk the shore
Together

Evermore

You may

Put eye to the sky
And go a field,

Place your hands
Within
Their earthly origin;

But still
Something's
Concealed.

No Longer Running

I ran out to get it
But, it was gone.
And I wondered

Was I too slow,
Was it not meant to be,
Was it faster than me.

Obviously,
All three.

Now I see
The lesson be
I no longer run
To find destiny.

Moments

Living in

The multitude
     of variations
Known as

In between.

The View

Looking through,
Reflecting you;

Windows
In the dark

Are mirrors too.

Clocks and Faces

All of a Sudden

The encounter
Took a fiery start;
We went away loved.

In the time we had
We offered one another
What the moments
Had to give
But, wanted more.

The bliss,
That at times,
Seemed like forever,
Went too fast.

The parting was sudden:
A handful of evenings
Too short.
But, all life is
All of a sudden.

Momentarily

It will be
A different highway
For you my friend.

Though
The same
In that
We're both
On the
Way.

Nonetheless,

A way
Shaped
Differently
For you
And for me
If only
Momentarily.

La Femme

Femme,
Are you
        by chance
The eternity
I see
In lovers eyes?

Is your forever
Giving

The truth
Of living?

Let's Start

Let's
Embrace
In the thin of air
Between our hearts

Never to part

Let's start

Loving

Self Portraits

In the mirrored hall
Of the mind
We find

That

Which
Was never lost.

The cost -
The going.

Ineffable

Me
    Reaching
    To you
    As dawn
    Reaches
    To light

You
    Reaching
    To me
    As light
    Reaches
    To dawn

Tick-n-Tock

Darkness,
What of light
If not silhouetted
Against the grace

Of your subtle shades.

What Last

The sun moves
Over the glass,
It's not moving slow,
It's not moving fast.

A shadow is cast,
It grows tall
Then it grows small.
Then

There's no shadow
At all.

What last?

Equilibrium

Between
Me and you,

Letting go
Is an illusion
And holding on
Is too.

There You Go

The evenings are
Still evenings;

The days
Still days.

Winter will come
And the birds,
And the leaves,
And the long
Sunny days
Will go away.

Everyone
And everything
Goes away
Sooner or
Later.

You went away
And that's okay.

Best Friends

On one cold night
Speaking words of comfort
Love befriended me
Saying softly,

"So what of this winter
From which the robins
Have flown.

Cardinals
Bright in flight
Still dart
From tree to tree.

And chattering sparrows
Chirp
Contently.

Come lovingly close
And be
A friend to me."

That
That Last

For all the distance gone
We can't be
Any further
Than where we are.

Between
To be

And
Has been

There's you and me.

Truth
Never comes to know
Destiny.
And how possibly
The past.

For it's now
That last.

Boundless

One
Is an illusion

Two
Is humankinds
Greatest dilemma

Balance

Knowing
The day
As we know
The night

Knowing
Dark
As we know
Light

In Moments: This to the Next

No Moments Captured

O how wondrously
The flame flickers

Before it goes out

The next moment.

Live full.

Time –
And You and Me

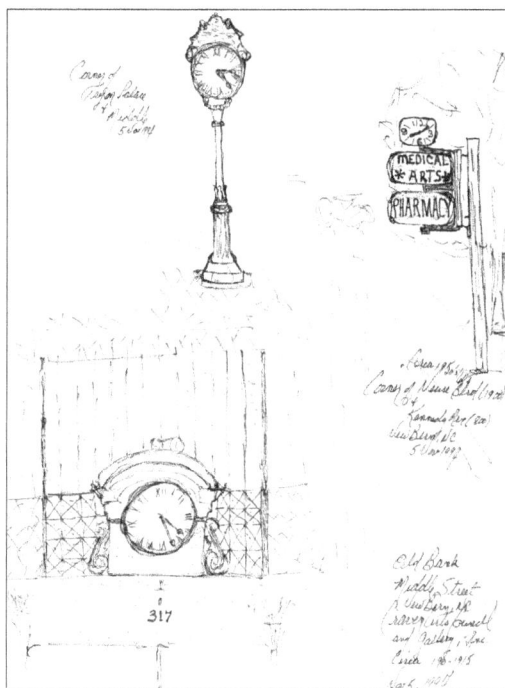

Where Will You Be

Where will you be
the minute
after
the last minute
of
eternity. . .

In the Balance

Morning,
Glancing this way,
Awoke
Blue sky day.

Hours were spent.
People went
Hither then thither,
Searching
Then discovering
Multitude
In dichotomy.

In it all
Did I miss something?

Perhaps,
Perhaps not.

Harmony

Knowing the universe
As the universe
Knows me;
Harmony.

In Moments: This to the Next

Golden

1

So wonderful
Youth
Fresh-with-free-ness.

Forever drunk
On the glow
Of the ring
Of the moon
And the red of wine.

2

How delightful
Summer sausage
And cheese
Wine as you please;
The open air café,
And the nights lived through
Till the break of day.

3

So wonderful
Youth
And ever more so
The days that flow
From spring
Through summer
Then fall,
Which all
Unfold
A gift of gold
As we
Grow old.

Tranquility

In the world of going
We go

In the world of generation
We sow

In the world of colors
We see

In the world of tranquility
We Be

In Moments: This to the Next

The Way

Be
Not the moment,
Nor the hour,
Nor the day;
But,
The way -
Love.

Day to Day

1

There are those
                who
Know the hands
            of mid-night
Like
The back of their hand.

And those
Who know noon
By the mid-day sun.

Venturing,
Everyone.

2

Some lives
Are short
   by count,

Some long;

In the greater
Measure

No count
Being right
No count
Being wrong.

And so it goes

Day-to-day.

Cipher

No matter
what the
challenge
the password is
Love.

The Loving Heart

The place

That knows not
The sands of time

Nor a space
Called empty, full
Or in between

That place

The Loving Heart

For Time's Sake

Teardrops,
Then rivers,
Then the sea

The crying
Of all of you
And me
Too

With an eye
To weep away
The heartfelt
Taken by the day

All
For time's sake

Eddies of Leaves

All of us

Leaves

Hanging on
Or having fallen from
Wind tossed trees.

Between the spring breeze
And the fall winds

Leaves,
Be they spring green
Or fall brown,
Get knocked around
While holding on
Or while whirling about
In eddies of leaves.

Rocked

Cradled
In the arms
That mark the minutes
And mark the hours,

That mark the days,
The years,
And millennia too;

Here

Rocked,
By times lullaby,
You and I,

We come together
Quietly
For what noise
Could there be
In such harmony.

Mt. Kumjong

The brook
Running down
Mt. Kumjong
And past Pomosa
Babbles, rushes,
And darts.

Talkative,
It speaks of centuries
Long before temple bells.

It talks of winged birds,
Leafy trees,
Of sunrise
And sunset.

And today
As it flows
It speaks of these yet.

To Love

No hands
Be they yours,
Mine,
Or those of time

Can touch as tenderly
As the hands
Of Love.

Be open
To Love.

Sailing

Somewhere
In the sky

The blue
Turns into you

So Much
For Time

Wherever you are
Whenever then is

Will be now.

At One With

You stepped into my eyes

And me
　　　into yours.

To There

Someday
            in age
There'll be
      not a season

And that's okay.

Come with me:
Carefree
To there.

In Moments: This To the Next

ABOUT THE AUTHOR

Inspired by nature and the beauty around him
Gary W. Burns started writing poetry at a young age.
Early on Gary was able to express his thoughts, ideas
and emotions through the vivid imagery of his verse.
His poetry has been published in various literary arts
journals, anthologies and magazines. He is the author
of 10 books of poetry. Through his poems Gary
shares his reflections on the many facets of life and
on the beauty of nature. The expressiveness of his
poetry has been enriched by his wide reading in
philosophy and psychology. He has traveled
throughout the world and has lived in numerous
countries, to include, Italy, Korea, Saudi Arabia and
Canada. He has also lived in Hawaii and several
other states. Currently, Gary makes his home in
Northern Virginia near the foothills of the Blue Ridge
Mountains.

ENJOY THESE OTHER BOOKS OF POETRY BY GARY W. BURNS

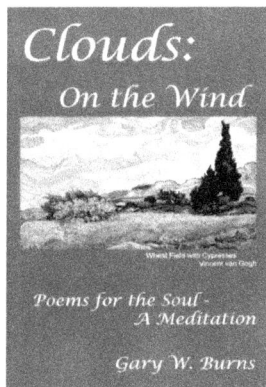

Clouds: On the Wind
(Poems for the Soul – A Meditation)
ISBN: 978-0-9845342-0-2 (Paperback)
ISBN: 978-0-9845342-1-0 (Hardcover)
ISBN: 978-0-986090-3-5 (E-Book)

Bridges: To There
(Poems for the Mind, Body & Spirit)
ISBN: 978-0-9827805-6-5 (Paperback)
ISBN: 978-0-9827805-7-2 (Hardcover)
ISBN: 978-0-9860900-4-2 (E-Book)

Earth Tones: A Journey
(Poetry for the Journey)
ISBN: 978-0-9845342-6-5 (Paperback)
ISBN: 978-0-9845342-9-6 (Hardcover)
ISBN: 978-0-9860900-8-0 (E-Book)

Available at WWW.TURNINGCORNERBOOKS.COM and where books are sold.

Dawn
and Beyond:
A Serenade

Poetry to Harmony
Gary W. Burns

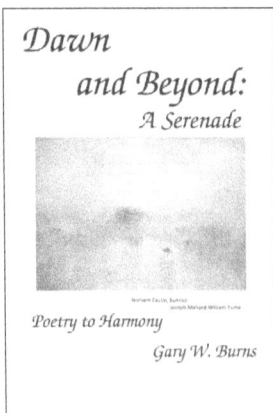

Dawn and Beyond: A Serenade
(Poetry to Harmony) (Due Out)
ISBN: 978-0-9827805-8-9 (Paperback)
ISBN: 978-0-9827805-9-6 (Hardcover)

Garden Walks:
Hand In Hand

Poems To Relax By
Gary W. Burns

Garden Walks: Hand In Hand
(Poems To Relax By)
ISBN: 978-0-9845342-3-4 (Paperback)
ISBN: 978-0-9827805-0-3 (Hardcover)
ISBN: 978-0-9860900-1-1 (E-Book)

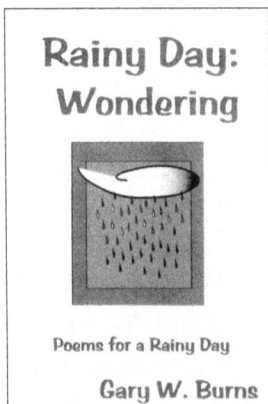

Rainy Day:
Wondering

Poems for a Rainy Day
Gary W. Burns

Rainy Day: Wondering
(Poetry for a Rainy Day)
ISBN: 978-0-9845342-5-8 (Paperback)
ISBN: 978-0-9827805-2-7 (Hardcover)
ISBN: 978-0-9860900-7-3 (E-Book)

Available at WWW.TURNINGCORNERBOOKS.COM and where books are sold.

To You With Love: Selected Poems
ISBN: 978-0-9845342-6-5 (Paperback)
ISBN: 978-0-9827805-3-4 (Hardcover)
ISBN: 978-0-9860900-2-8 (E-Book)

Twilight: Awaking the Stars
(Poems of the Night's Light)
ISBN: 978-0-9845342-7-2 (Paperback)
ISBN: 978-0-9827805-4-1 (Hardcover)
ISBN: 978-0-9860900-6-6 (E-Book)

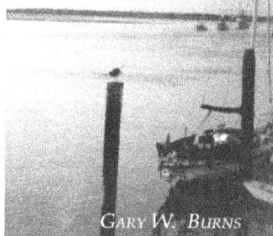

Poems of Love: A Selection
ISBN: 978-0-9845342-8-9 (Paperback)
ISBN: 978-0-9827805-5-8 (Hardcover)
ISBN: 978-0-9860900-5-9 (E-Book)

Available at WWW.TURNINGCORNERBOOKS.COM and where books are sold.

www.ingramcontent.com/pod-product-compliance
Lightning Source LLC
Chambersburg PA
CBHW021837020426
42334CB00014B/666